CASSIE'S SOAP OPERA

CASSIE'S SOAP OPERA

by
JOHN ESCOTT
Illustrated by Kate Rogers

HAMISH HAMILTON
LONDON

First published in Great Britain 1986
by Hamish Hamilton Children's Books
Garden House   57–59 Long Acre   London WC2E 9JZ
Copyright © 1986 by John Escott
Illustrations copyright © 1986 by Kate Rogers

British Library Cataloguing in Publication Data
Escott, John
    Cassie's soap opera.—(Antelope books)
    I. Title II. Rogers, Kate
    823'.914[J]   PZ7

    ISBN 0 241 11860 3

Filmset in Baskerville by
Katerprint Co. Ltd, Oxford
Printed in Great Britain at the
Univesity Press, Cambridge

Chapter 1

CASSIE sat cross-legged on the floor in front of the TV and blinked in admiration. On screen, Desma Blane's tanned face froze as the familiar sound of the *Blane's Park* signature tune filled the headphones over Cassie's ears.

"Cassie!"

Her mother's voice pierced the sound of the music as Cassie pushed the rewind button on the video. She pulled the headphones plug from the TV and turned round.

Mrs Bond was sitting up in bed, her nightie crumpled so that the Snoopy face on the front looked in pain. "You do realise what time it is, don't you?"

Cassie glanced at the figures of the digital clock-radio on the table between her mother's bed and her own. "Six-o-two."

"In the morning," her mother reminded her. "What have you been watching, for heaven's sake?"

2

"Last night's *Blane's Park*. You made me go to bed early, remember? I had to record it."

"And you just watched the whole thirty minutes now?"

"Yes."

"Which means you must have got up at five-thirty." Mrs Bond sighed. "At least you didn't wake me. Let's hope you didn't wake the rest of the hotel either."

"I used headphones," Cassie told her.

"I hope it was worth it," Mrs Bond said.

Cassie's face lit up. "Oh, it was. Desma Blane wants the building where Tabitha Slygh runs her fashion business, and Desma had just worked out a plan to get it away from Tabitha and

3

make a million dollars at the same time. She plans to —"

"Stop, I don't want to hear." Mrs Bond pushed a hand through her thick fair hair. "It's too complicated for this time of day."

There was a coffee-making machine next to the clock-radio and Cassie's mother switched it on before swinging her legs over the side of the bed. Cassie watched as she crossed to the bath-room.

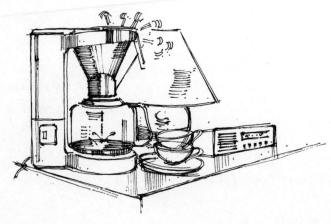

All the *Hotel Barton* rooms had bath-rooms attached – *en suite*, as the brochure said. The fact that they were barely large enough to accommodate the toilet, washbasin and shower didn't stop Cassie being impressed. She and her mother certainly weren't used to this style of living.

But the biggest delight had been the colour TV and video. Back in their flat, where the lease had run out just two days after her mother had got this job, Cassie had been forced to watch her beloved soap operas on a portable black-and-white.

She watched them all, but her favourite was the twice-weekly American saga, *Blane's Park*, in which Desma Blane, property tycoon, wheeled and dealed against the glamorous background of the Californian sunshine. Every Monday and Tuesday evening, Cassie wallowed in it, unless forced to record it as she had been last night.

One day, Cassie promised herself, she would go to California.

Mrs Bond came back from the bathroom and poured out some coffee. She could look quite beautiful if she tried, Cassie thought. If she let her hair grow and got a sunlamp, then worked at some exercises, why she'd look a bit like Tabitha Slygh.

"Coffee?"

"No, thanks," Cassie said. "I had some orange juice earlier."

Her mother kept a few odd items for snacks in the room, but they ate most of their meals in the hotel restaurant. *Had* eaten them, Cassie reminded herself silently. But not for much longer.

They had been here since the beginning of May, six months now, but Mrs Bond's job – sorting out the accounts books before the hotel was sold – was almost finished and they would be moving on. Cassie didn't know where, and didn't think her mother knew either.

"You watch too much TV," Mrs Bond said, sipping her coffee and looking for a biscuit to nibble.

Cassie handed her the tin from the floor where she'd been eating and watching *Blane's Park* at the same time.

"It's educational."

"Not the rubbish you watch," Mrs Bond said.

Cassie went to the window and pulled back the curtains. Their room, five floors up, overlooked a narrow alleyway at the rear of the hotel, where the delivery vans unloaded. It was still dark outside. There was a warehouse opposite and, apart from a lighted doorway where a nightwatchman stood reading a newspaper, that too was in darkness.

"Anybody would think we didn't

have enough excitement in our own lives," Mrs Bond went on. "Living from hand to mouth."

It was a joke, of course. Things weren't quite as bad as that. Freelance book-keeping was a slightly uncertain way to make a living but Mrs Bond was good at her job. Since Cassie's father had died, four years ago, she had managed to earn enough to support herself and her daughter even if it was only with difficulty sometimes.

Their furniture was in store, awaiting a new flat or even some sort of house, but that depended on Mrs Bond's next job.

"What happens when you finish here?" Cassie asked, forcing herself to admit that this *Blane's Park*-style of living couldn't go on forever.

9

Mrs Bond grinned. "I was wondering when you'd get around to asking. I know you're going to hate leaving here, but we have to. At the end of the week, as it happens."

Cassie gulped. "That soon? But – but have you found another job?"

Mrs Bond drained the last of her coffee and stretched back against the velvet headboard. "As a matter of fact, I have."

Cassie went over and sat on her mother's duvet. "Which part of the city will we be living in this time? I hope it's somewhere nice, I'd hate it if – "

Mrs Bond put an arm around her daughter's shoulder.

(*Like the scene where Tabitha Slygh is told her mother has lost her fortune. When Tabitha says, bravely, "You'll just have to make another million, Mummy." And Mrs Slygh replies, "I'm too sick to do that now, Tabitha. You must do it for me.")*

"Not in the city at all, actually," Mrs Bond said.

Cassie looked astonished. "Where then?"

"Hartleigh Heights," her mother said. "Where Aunt Bridget and Uncle Guy live."

Aunt Bridget and Uncle Guy. Names on Christmas cards. Hartleigh Heights; just a postmark.

"Where will *we* live?"

"A cottage. One of three belonging to Uncle Guy. They're holiday cottages but, being November, they're empty."

Cassie had forgotten Hartleigh Heights was on the coast. "Is that what Uncle Guy does? Own holiday cottages?"

"And an estate agency," her mother said.

"Estate agency? You mean buying and selling houses?"

"For other people," her mother said. "Although I believe Guy owns one or two other properties besides the cottages. I think he's made quite a bit of money out of it."

(*"There's money in property,"* Desma Blane *said almost every week.*)

"What about school?" Cassie asked.

"You'll go to the local one," her mother said. "It's only for six months, probably. The woman who looks after Uncle Guy's accounts is having a baby and has had to stop work until the Spring. I'll be filling in until then."

Changing schools didn't bother Cassie too much. It wouldn't be the first time. Moving around, the way her mother's work meant they had to, had caused it to happen before. And Cassie was a solitary sort of person anyway, as her mother was always saying, actually

13

preferring her own company to being part of a crowd. She knew more about Desma Blane and Tabitha Slygh than she did about any of the children at school.

No, it was leaving the hotel that bothered her. And for some crummy cottage.

"They're looking forward to seeing you," Mrs Bond said. "Especially Aunt Bridget."

Aunt Bridget had stayed overnight once, just after Cassie's father had died. Cassie had a vague memory of her as somebody with a loud laugh.

She had never met Uncle Guy. Yet, in a way, he sounded interesting. Cottages, other properties, an estate agency. Not exactly Desma Blane, property tycoon, but still . . .

Chapter 2

THEY DROVE to Hartleigh Heights the following Sunday, the beginning of half-term holiday week. The town was all hills, the buildings mostly grey and old, and everywhere smelled of seaweed.

"What a pongy place!" Cassie complained.

Uncle Guy owned three out of four cottages that stood at the end of an unmade road called Wesley Close. They were painted white and looked neat enough.

15

Which was more than could be said
for the fourth cottage at the end. This
had flaking paintwork and a slate roof
that sat on it like a crumpled hat.

*(Like the fisherman's cottage where Desma
Blane's stepson hid after escaping from
prison.)*

The cottages had gardens which
backed on to a cemetery. Cassie turned

up her nose. "Nice cheerful view," she said, but her mother ignored her.

But beyond the rows of pale head-stones, the fields swept up to the cliffs and you could see the sea, fulfilling the claims made by the cottage's name, *Seavista*.

Inside everything was reversed, the living room and kitchen upstairs with the better view, the two bedrooms and miniature bathroom downstairs.

It wasn't the *Hotel Barton* that was for sure, Cassie thought.

Then her mother pointed to something in the corner of the living room. "That should please you, anyway."

It was a portable colour television.

Cassie smiled.

It was a grey afternoon with a faint mist out to sea. Cassie spent it mooching about the back garden. In the cemetery a bonfire burned in one corner. A man with a wheelbarrow fed it with dead leaves, helped by a tall, skinny boy of about Cassie's age who was raking between the gravestones and emptying the litter baskets.

Later, when the blaze had died

down, both of them went through the garden gate of the fourth cottage. They left the wheelbarrow on the garden path and entered a lean-to building at the back of the cottage. A light went on and Cassie saw them moving about inside.

After a while, she went back indoors. Mrs Bond had put on lights because the afternoon had slipped away.

Aunt Bridget had invited them for a meal that evening and, later on, as Mrs Bond's tiny car wound through Hartleigh's narrow streets, Cassie decided they were the poor relations accepting the charity of their rich relatives. Now which series had that come from?

The fantasy became more real when Mrs Bond turned the car into a wide driveway and they saw the impressive white house at the end.

"Wow!" Cassie said. "I didn't realise Uncle Guy was a millionaire."

Her mother laughed but was obviously just as surprised. "They must have a spectacular view of the harbour in daylight."

An outside light like a large coaching lamp threw a pool of yellow over the

steps up to the front door. In the drive
stood a dark blue Mercedes saloon.

The front door opened and Uncle
Guy came down the steps to greet them.
He was a tall man wearing a brown
suit, a brown shirt and a cream-col-
oured tie. His hair looked as though it
had just been blow-dried and, when he
smiled, he reminded Cassie of Desma
Blane's first husband who had been
jailed for fraud.

"So this is Cassie," he said after kissing Mrs Bond on the cheek. Cassie smelled after-shave when he gave her a hug.

"How is Bridget," Mrs Bond asked.

"Fine, Liz. Just fine. Come inside, she's waiting for you."

The hall was panelled in dark wood with four large paintings of bullfighters hanging around it. A thick, purple-patterned carpet deadened their footsteps as they crossed to the living room, which was almost as large as the lounge at the *Hotel Barton*, Cassie discovered. The furniture was big and heavy and expensive-looking, and there were patio doors at the end, leading on to a terrace.

In almost every American soap saga that Cassie had watched (and there had been an awful lot), the hero or heroine's house always had a terrace. And a swimming pool.

It was too dark outside to see if Uncle Guy had a swimming pool.

Even Aunt Bridget with her sleek clothes and swept-up hairstyle looked as though she'd just stepped out of *Blane's Park*.

"Hallo, Cassie." She gave Cassie a wet, slightly sticky kiss, then said, "Come on, we can eat straight away."

The dining room had a long, polished table with hunting-scene placemats and no tablecloth. The meal – some sort of beef thing – was hot and spicy and Cassie had to drink four glasses of water to get it down. The pudding, Devil's Foodcake, was rich and tangy as well so that her stomach felt as if it had been attacked by a flame-thrower by the time she'd finished.

But Cassie was impressed.

This was how you lived when you were rich and successful. The setting reminded her so much of a scene from *Blane's Park* it was almost creepy. And Uncle Guy, sitting there smoking a cigar, could easily have been a character from the series.

"How do you like the cottage, Liz?" Aunt Bridget asked.

"Lovely," Mrs Bond said. "Look, we really appreciate —"

Uncle Guy held up a hand. "Please, say no more. You're doing me a favour."

"Pretty cottages, aren't they?" Aunt Bridget said.

"I bought them last year," Uncle Guy explained. "Before the season

began. They belonged to a woman who lived in one and rented out the other two. I got them when she died, then managed to ease out the other tenants so that I could convert the cottages for holiday letting. Much more profitable that way."

"What about the fourth one at the end of the row?" Mrs Bond asked.

Uncle Guy frowned. "Sore point, I'm afraid. An old chap had it for years, then died suddenly. Now a man lives there with his son. McNeil, their name is."

"Why a sore point?"

"I want that other cottage, Liz. For the land, to build on. The three are a reasonable little investment, but with the whole piece of land I could knock them down and build four times as

27

many holiday chalets. That's more profit."

"But Mr McNeil won't sell?"

"Right. I've made several very fair offers, considering the state the place is in, but he won't budge. Not that I've given up, quite. There may be other ways of persuading him."

Cassie listened intently. You could see why Uncle Guy was rich. He had the same determined look about him that Desma Blane had as she wheeled and dealed twice-weekly. You got the feeling that, like her, once Uncle Guy's mind was made up, nothing would stop him.

(*"I don't take no for an answer,"* Desma Blane said. *"I take it as a challenge."*)

Cassie was curious about the McNeil man as well. Later, when they arrived back at Wesley Close, she glanced at the lighted downstairs window of the fourth cottage and wondered. Wondered what sort of person said "no" to Uncle Guy. She had the feeling not many people did that.

Chapter 3

THE FOLLOWING MORNING Mrs Bond left early for Uncle Guy's office.

"You'll be all right, won't you?" she asked Cassie.

"Of course," Cassie told her. "I might go for a walk later."

A pale sun had emerged from behind grey-tipped clouds and there were chunks of blue sky the colour of faded jeans. In the distance, the sea's surface was speckled with white tips. It looked more like April than November, Cassie thought.

She dressed and put on a thick jacket before going out. She was glad of it, she found, as the wind was chillier than expected, coming straight off the cold surface of the sea.

There was a path which went along the edge of the cemetery, leading to the cliff top. Cassie began to make her way past the gravestones.

Mr McNeil was pruning a tree which overhung the path. He was up a ladder using a large D-shaped saw. Farther along the path, making a fresh bonfire with the cuttings from the tree, was the boy Cassie had seen the day before.

"Hang on, Dad," the boy called. "Somebody coming."

"Right, Paul." Mr McNeil stopped

sawing as Cassie passed underneath the tree. He gave her a smile. "Morning, nice day."

"Good morning," Cassie said. "Yes, it is."

She moved out from under the tree and the man took it as a signal to begin sawing again. When Cassie drew level with Paul McNeil, the boy stopped what he was doing and stared at her. Cassie felt forced to speak, uncomfortable under the stare.

"Hallo," she said.

He nodded. "At one of the cottages, are you?"

"That's right."

"Bit late for a holiday, isn't it?"

Cassie was taken aback by the abruptness of the question. "We – we're just staying there for the moment."

He gave another nod, seemed about to speak again but then turned away and went back to his work. Cassie walked on.

"Enjoy your walk," he called after her when she'd gone a little way.

She turned to reply and found him not looking at her but grinning to himself. For some reason this annoyed her. She felt her cheeks go red, and for the rest of the way along the cemetery path she was certain he was watching her.

She would come back the road way, she decided.

The beach, when she found it, was a stretch of gritty-grey shingle flecked with seaweed and bits of wood. A few other people were about, mostly walking dogs, but two boys came across the water on small sailing dinghies, one

more accomplished than the other.
They touched down on the beach only
briefly before setting off again, the
second boy grappling with the sail as he
tried to reboard.

The wind whipped across Cassie's

face, stinging her cheeks and ears. She turned away from the sea and looked up the sloping beach to a road which wound upwards between tiers of houses, some with breathtaking views of the bay and coastline. Most had terraces and balconies.

And one of them gleamed whiter-than-white, the way Uncle Guy's house had when Cassie and her mother had approached it the night before. And there were the patio doors overlooking the terrace. It had to be the same one.

From here, the resemblance to Desma Blane's mansion was so strong it was spooky. Except that Desma's home was cut into the side of a cliff overlooking the Pacific ocean.

Perhaps if they stayed here long enough, Cassie thought, she and her mother might end up with one of those houses. Maybe Uncle Guy would show her mother how to make a lot of money; buying and selling properties, perhaps.

It might be nice to live by the sea. Already the pongy seaweedy smell seemed much less noticeable. Cassie considered it as she walked.

But it was too cold to walk for long and Cassie soon turned and retraced her steps back up the cliff path and across the fields to the cemetery. Remembering what she'd decided earlier, she avoided the cemetery path and went round to the road and Wesley Close.

Almost the first thing she saw was Uncle Guy's blue Mercedes. It was standing outside the McNeil cottage. Cassie went past, trying not to look too curious, and let herself into *Seavista*.

Was Uncle Guy having one more try at persuading Mr McNeil to sell?

She took off her coat and went to

make a warm drink. As she filled the kettle at the sink, Cassie glanced out of the kitchen window at the Close below. Uncle Guy had emerged from the end cottage and was getting into his car.

He didn't look pleased.

On that evening's episode of *Blane's Park*, Desma Blane was outwitted by Tabitha Slygh and lost half a million dollars. She didn't look pleased either.

Cassie's mother was stretched out on the couch reading a paperback. "Honestly, Cass, I don't know how you can watch that junk."

"It's not junk," Cassie said. She switched off the TV as the episode ended. "It's all about big business, tycoons, that sort of thing."

She walked over to the window and

looked out. Darkness. Not a star in the sky, no moon. Just the light in the lean-to building at the back of Mr McNeil's cottage. Cassie wondered what he kept in there.

"I saw Uncle Guy coming away from the McNeil cottage earlier," she told her mother.

Mrs Bond looked up. "You did? He said he was going to call again. I wonder if Mr McNeil has changed his mind about selling?"

"Going by the look on Uncle Guy's face as he came out, I shouldn't think so," Cassie said.

"I can't see him giving up yet," Mrs Bond said.

Nor can I, Cassie thought.

Chapter 4

"MEET ME at the office at lunchtime, Cassie," Mrs Bond said. "Get some rolls or something and we'll eat on the quayside."

The freakish weather – more sun and blue sky – made a nonsense of the fact that it was November. The morning was Springlike and tempting enough for Cassie's mother to suggest eating out-doors.

"All right," Cassie said. "I was going to look round the town anyway."

She washed up her breakfast things after Mrs Bond had left the cottage. Looking out of the kitchen window, she could see Mr McNeil up a ladder again, this time working on an oak tree in the far corner of the cemetery. Cemetery caretaker seemed an odd sort of job for a youngish man, Cassie thought.

Half an hour later when she went out, Paul McNeil was leaning against the gate of the fourth cottage eating an apple.

"More walking?" he said as she drew level.

"I thought I'd take a look at the town," Cassie said.

He laughed shortly. "You'll be back in no time, then." He bit into his apple again, chewed it for several seconds, then said, "Didn't know Mr Guy Kes-

wick did Winter lettings." He spoke the
name mockingly.

Cassie decided there was no point in
keeping secrets, the truth would come
out in the end. "He – he's my uncle,
actually. My mother has come here to
work for him."

He didn't look in the least surprised, just nodded and said, "We thought it was probably something like that," a note of sourness in his voice.

"We?"

"Dad and me." He chewed some more of his apple whilst Cassie stared awkwardly across the cemetery at Mr McNeil clambering amongst the big branches of the oak tree.

"Well," she said. "I'll be going on."

"You know your uncle wants Dad to sell him our cottage, don't you?" Paul said abruptly.

Cassie looked at him. "He . . . said something about it."

Paul gave a grunt. "I'll bet he did! But Dad won't sell, see? Your precious uncle can get as mad as he likes!"

"It – it's nothing to do with me,"

44

Cassie said, but she felt angry at being spoken to in this way. "But I can't see why your father's so keen to stay. The roof looks as though it could collapse any second."

He threw the apple core over his shoulder, his face turning scarlet. "Yes, well we aren't all millionaires like your uncle —"

"He's not a millionaire, don't be stupid."

"Well, he certainly acts like one —"

"Anyway, if he offered your dad a fair price —"

"You don't know anything about it," the boy snapped. "Money! That's all Keswick is interested in, isn't it? And I suppose you're the same being a relative. Well, there are other things."

"I didn't say – " Cassie began.

"For one thing," Paul swept on, ignoring her interruption, "the cottage belonged to my great uncle, and Dad doesn't think he would have liked us to sell it just because *your* uncle offers us a fancy price."

"I didn't know – " Cassie said.

"No, you didn't, did you? And I don't suppose you care, either." He stopped, as if all the anger had suddenly been drained out of him; as if

46

he was slightly ashamed of the way he had sounded off.

There was an embarrassed silence and the two of them looked everywhere but at each other. Cassie had been astonished at the anger but, at the same time, had a sneaking admiration for the way he stood up for himself and his father and what they felt.

Cassie was the one who finally broke the silence. "Your dad looks after the cemetery all the time?"

He looked relieved that the tension had been broken. "Yes. It was what my great uncle did before he died. When he left Dad the cottage in his will, Dad decided to come and live here rather than sell the place, and he took on the job as well."

"I see," Cassie said.

"Not quite, you don't," Paul said. "My dad worked in a factory but hated it, and he had this hobby which he did evenings and weekends."

"Hobby?"

Paul hesitated, then nodded towards the lean-to building at the back of the cottage. "Come on, I'll show you. Dad won't mind." He led the way through the gate and up the garden path, Cassie following. "The hobby's become more a sort of job now," Paul said, "and that's one of the reasons Dad took this place and the cemetery job, to give him more time to do it."

He opened the door of the lean-to and they went inside. There was a bench, a lathe, tool racks fixed to the walls in neat rows, a shelf of paints and varnishes, and a long table which served as a drying area for the results of Mr McNeil's work.

Cassie stared at the objects on the table. "Your dad makes *toys*?"

Paul grinned at her surprise. "Mostly. Plus some wood carvings."

Cassie looked at the wooden models – steam engines, fire engines, cars, trucks, boats, aeroplanes – all painted in bright colours or varnished to a glossy shine.

"And it all began as a hobby?" Cassie said.

"That's right," Paul said. "Then he began to sell some to people who wanted to give them as presents. After that, it grew and grew, but it's only since we came here that he's been turning it into a proper little business. Of course, we don't have much to live on until things get going." He gave her a half-smile. "That's why the roof hasn't been repaired."

"Look, I didn't mean – "

"It's all right," he said. "I – I'm sorry I blew up earlier. It's just that I get mad whenever I think of your uncle trying to force us out."

Cassie picked up a fire engine. It was beautifully made. "Where does your father sell them?"

"There's a shop in town that buys from him, especially in the summer when the visitors are here. And he goes to craft and toy fairs."

They went back into the garden when Cassie had finished looking around. Paul nodded towards the shed in the corner. "That's where we store most of the wood." In the opposite corner stood a motorcycle and sidecar. "He uses that for taking stuff to exhibitions and fairs."

"Your dad sounds well organised," Cassie said.

"He is now," Paul said. "It's just the money that's the problem. But things will sort themselves out." He looked directly at Cassie, as if giving her a message to pass on. "We won't be beaten."

And that, Cassie thought a little later when she was making her way towards the town, was exactly what a competitor of Desma Blane's had said a few episodes ago.

Just before Desma put him out of business.

Chapter 5

THE OFFICE BELONGING to Uncle Guy
was on the quayside, at the corner of a
road with a cobbled surface. Cassie
went in the door and was confronted by
a plump woman with purple hair. She
sat behind a desk with a typewriter on it
and looked up as Cassie entered.

"Hallo, dearie. You're Cassie, are
you?" Even as she said this, she was
looking out of the window and typing at
the same time. The window was full of

53

photographs of Hartleigh Heights properties that were for sale.

"Yes," Cassie said. The purple hair, she guessed, was really grey underneath.

"Thought you must be. I'm Miss Cartwright." She laughed. "Or Miss Cartwheel, as Mr Keswick sometimes calls me."

Cassie smiled politely. "Where is my mother?"

"In the back room, dearie," Miss Cartwright said.

Cassie looked past her towards an open door where her mother sat at a desk, fingers tapping away at an adding machine. There was another room next to it with the words "Guy Keswick" painted on the frosted glass door. The door was open and the room empty.

"Hallo, Cass," Mrs Bond said, looking up as her daughter came in. "Had a look round the town?"

Cassie sat down in a chair beside her mother's desk. "Mm."

"What did you think of it?"

Cassie shrugged, conscious of the ears of Miss Cartwright who had stopped typing for a moment. "All right," she said. In fact, the shops were cramped and cluttered but the people had been friendly enough, chatting about the good weather and asking if she was on holiday. They had known she was a stranger and Cassie supposed it was her city accent that gave her away. It was something she would have to watch when she began school again. No doubt the local kids would make fun of her.

"Did you bring some rolls?" Mrs Bond asked.

"Yes." Cassie began to fish around in her shopping carrier.

"It's all right," Mrs Bond said, "we'll go and sit in the sun. It's warmer today."

Miss Cartwright gave them a toothy smile as they passed her desk.

"Aren't you going for lunch, Miss Cartwright?" Mrs Bond asked.

"Later, dearie. I want to wait for Mr Keswick, he should be back soon."

Cassie and her mother went out on to the quayside. They found a seat by the war memorial and Cassie took rolls and a flask of coffee from the shopping bag. Gulls whirled overhead and a small boat chugged away from the quayside making a fan-shaped pattern in the water behind it.

"I saw Paul McNeil earlier," Cassie said, biting into a cheese-and-tomato roll.

"Paul McNeil?"

"The boy at the cottage Uncle Guy wants to buy."

"Ah, yes," Mrs Bond said. "What's he like?"

Cassie remembered Paul's burst of anger but said, "He's OK, really." Then added, "He knows who we are, that Uncle Guy is related."

"Well, I don't suppose that matters. What Uncle Guy does is his business."

Cassie munched in silence for a while, then said, "Did you know that Mr McNeil makes toys?"

"Toys?" Mrs Bond said, surprised.

So Cassie told her about the workshop.

"Interesting," her mother said. "I wonder if Uncle Guy knows about it."

"The cottage belonged to Paul's

58

great uncle," Cassie went on. "It was left to Mr McNeil in the old man's will, which is one reason they don't want to sell."

Mrs Bond nodded thoughtfully. "I doubt if Uncle Guy knows that."

Cassie thought it would make little difference.

(*"You can't be sentimental in business,"* *Desma Blane said. She had just forced her own father to go broke to make certain her business was the biggest in the area.*)

"Is Uncle Guy a tycoon?" Cassie asked.

Mrs Bond laughed. "Well, I suppose you could call him that, but it seems a bit grand. Mind you, I rather suspect that's how Uncle Guy sees himself."

Cassie thought so as well.

They ate their lunch and watched more boats criss-crossing the water in front of them. Then, because she wanted to use the toilet, Cassie left her mother and went on back to the office ahead of her.

"It's through the door in the corner of the main office," Mrs Bond called after her. "Tell Miss Cartwright I'll be back shortly."

When Cassie reached the corner of the cobbled street, Uncle Guy's Mercedes was standing outside the office. As she drew closer, Cassie could see him inside, talking to Miss Cartwright.

They had their backs to the street and
didn't see Cassie in the doorway.

" . . . so I've given up making McNeil
offers," Uncle Guy was saying.

Cassie hesitated, knowing they
hadn't heard her and not wanting to be
caught eavesdropping but curious now
that she'd caught the name of Paul's
father.

"He doesn't sound as if he's going to move," Miss Cartwright said. "Not from what you've told me."

"Which is why this is the only answer," Uncle Guy replied.

"Quite," Miss Cartwright agreed. She looked as though she would agree with anything Uncle Guy said, Cassie thought.

"Thynners will certainly set things alight," Uncle Guy said. "And then – " He suddenly realised they weren't alone and turned to see Cassie in the doorway.

"Hallo," Cassie said, hurrying into the office now as if she'd only arrived that minute. "I – er – have to use the toilet." She passed quickly between them.

They were both smiling but Cassie

thought they looked startled as well.

And guilty?

It was Tabitha Slygh's funeral. Mourners were grouped around an open grave under a black umbrella, a light snow falling. In the background, unnoticed behind a snow-capped tombstone, stood the sinister but triumphant figure of Desma Blane watching her rival come to her final resting place.

Cassie stared unblinkingly at the TV screen as Tuesday night's episode of

Blane's Park came to an end. As Tabitha Slygh came to an end in fact. Desma Blane had got her revenge and her rival's business as well.

Cassie had known the character of Tabitha Slygh was going to die because she'd read it on the TV page of the Sunday newspaper several weeks ago. It was the only page Cassie ever looked at. In real life, the actress had wanted to come out of the series.

But Cassie hadn't expected such a shocking death for Tabitha – caught in a fire at the warehouse of her fashion business. A fire started by somebody paid by Desma Blane.

"Cass, it's time for bed," Mrs Bond said, awaking her daughter to the real world again.

"*Already?* Did you see that? Did you

see what happened to Tabitha?" Cassie said.

"Enough to give you nightmares," her mother said. "Go and read a nice book for five minutes before you go to sleep."

"You know TV doesn't scare me," Cassie scoffed.

And yet her heart *had* been beating like a tom-tom.

Chapter 6

CASSIE WOKE suddenly.

Her room was filled with a strange light, yet it couldn't be morning surely. She could only have been in bed a few hours. The moon? There'd been no moon earlier. Streetlamp? Her ground floor bedroom overlooked the back garden, not Wesley Close.

She pushed herself up on one elbow and looked towards the drawn curtains. Whatever the light was, it was *moving*.

66

Cassie's tom-tom heart began again. A torch? Somebody prowling in the back garden? Yet the light seemed more like a floodlight than a torch.

She forced herself to get out of bed and go to the window. Then, even before she drew back the curtains, she knew what the light was.

"A fire," she said aloud. "Somebody's having a bonfire."

In the middle of the night?

Cassie yanked back the curtains and saw flames shooting into the sky. Flames and smoke and sparks whirling above the hedge up the side of Mr McNeil's garden, so bright it was almost like daylight outside.

She grabbed her dressing gown and rushed into the tiny hallway, up the passage to the back door. "Mum!" she shouted, not waiting to see if her mother had heard and woken up.

The back door was open.

Taken aback, Cassie hesitated, then ran into the garden and down to the path at the edge of the cemetery.

"Cassie?" It was her mother, herself in dressing gown and slippers, face scrunched up against the heat of the fire.

Paul McNeil was standing beside her, hands pushed into the pockets of an anorak that had been hastily thrown over pyjamas.

"What is it burning?" Cassie shouted above the crackling and spitting sounds coming from the McNeil's garden.

"The shed," Paul told her. He spoke as though in his sleep, mesmerised by the fire. "All Dad's wood."

And there was not much of the shed left, Cassie saw now. It was almost at ground level, the fire actually dying down.

"The fire brigade are on their way," Mrs Bond said, "but they'll be too late to do anything except make sure the remains are properly damped down."

"Where's Mr McNeil?" Cassie asked. Then she saw him, standing in the shadows by the workshop, as if putting himself between the glowing menace and his precious toys.

The fire brigade arrived and did exactly what Cassie's mother had said they would. There wasn't much else to be done.

"How did it start?" Cassie asked.

"We don't know," Paul said.

"Vandals, I expect," Mrs Bond said.

71

"I suppose Hartleigh Heights has them like everywhere else. Mindless fools!"

"Or a cigarette end carelessly thrown over the hedge from the cemetery path," Paul said. "People do use it late at night, coming back from the town. The fire could have taken a little while to get going."

Mr McNeil joined them after the fire brigade had finished.

"Lucky it wasn't my workshop," he said. "That could have been much worse. All those tins of paint and thinners and varnish, the place would have gone up in no time."

Thinners.

The word echoed in Cassie's head like a large bell being struck.

"What – what's thinners?" she heard herself asking.

72

"It's the stuff you use to make paint go further," Paul explained. "Dad uses it for his models. You just have to be careful not to put it near a naked flame or it will catch alight at once."

"In fact," Mr McNeil said, "there was a can in the shed which explains why the place went up so quickly once the fire really started."

Thinners will certainly set things alight.

Uncle Guy's voice was so clear in Cassie's mind that she almost looked round expecting to see him standing beside her.

Chapter 7

ONE QUESTION.

One *enormous* question.

Did Uncle Guy set fire to Mr McNeil's shed?

Cassie sat up in her bed, toying with the bowl of cereal on the tray in front of her. Her mother had brought it to her before leaving for the office, thinking Cassie would want to lie in after their disturbed night.

Now, scraps of conversation floated in and out of Cassie's head.

"... *there may be other ways of persuading him ... I've given up making McNeil offers ... I don't take no for an answer, I take it as a challenge ...* " Wait a minute, that last bit belonged to Desma Blane not Uncle Guy. Uncle Guy ... Desma Blane ... property tycoons ... fires ... Everything was becoming confused, merging into one crazy, frightening picture.

She moved the tray and got out of bed. There was no sun today, just charcoal-grey clouds that lay low over the cliff-top. Cassie dressed and pulled on a topcoat before going outside into the back garden.

Thinners ... set things alight ...

Paul and his father were clearing up
some of the mess in their own garden
and Cassie almost went to see if she
could help, but then changed her mind.
With all the thoughts swirling around
in her head, it would be difficult not to
make her suspicions obvious to them.

Then, to her astonishment, she saw Uncle Guy – *with them*!

He was beside Mr McNeil, shaking his head as though shocked by what he saw, listening as Mr McNeil explained and pointed about with his arms.

What was Uncle Guy doing? Had he come to check the results? Had he come to make sure the fire had done its job?

Or was he making another offer for the cottage, now that Mr McNeil's supply of wood had been destroyed, now that his business had been severely damaged?

Hadn't Paul said there were money problems? Well, losing your stock of wood must be a major blow – and Uncle Guy would know that.

Cassie watched them for several minutes, shivering partly from cold,

partly from the thoughts in her head. Then Uncle Guy looked across the hedges and their eyes met. He gave a brief smile, waved, and went on talking to Mr McNeil.

Cassie went back indoors. She put the kettle on to make herself a cup of coffee, switched on the television for something to take her mind off things. It was some programme about tractors and she listened but didn't hear what the man in wellington boots was saying.

There was a knock at the door.

The kettle boiled at the same time but Cassie ignored it. She ignored the knocking as well, knowing who it would be.

"Cassie?"

The front door wasn't locked. Or he might have a key, she thought. After all, it was his cottage.

"Cassie, are you up there?"

There was no sense trying to hide the fact, he only had to walk up to find out. "Yes," she called down.

He came up. "All right?" he said, smiling.

Cassie avoided his eye. "Fine."

He sat on the couch. He was wearing a biscuit-coloured suit today, a chocolate brown handkerchief in the top pocket, sprouting like a flower in full bloom. "I've been talking to Mr McNeil. Dreadful business that fire of his."

(*"Dreadful," Desma Blane said after the fire at Tabitha Slygh's warehouse, knowing all the while that she'd paid somebody to set fire to it.*)

"The fire brigade think it was prob-

80

ably a cigarette end that started it,"
Uncle Guy said.

How could he act so cool? How could
he just *sit* there?

"Anyway," Uncle Guy went on after
a few moments during which Cassie
said nothing, "Mr McNeil's agreed to a
suggestion I've made."

Here it comes, Cassie thought. He's
now going to tell me that Mr McNeil
has finally been beaten, that he's agreed

to sell the cottage. Well he's not going to get it! Not like that, he isn't.

"He's agreed to see Thynners," Uncle Guy said.

Thinners . . .

"Thinners?" Cassie echoed, her voice sounding faraway. "*See* thinners?"

Uncle Guy nodded. "Mike Thynners, my accountant. You see, Mr McNeil is trying to set up a business and he needs some sound financial advice – where to raise capital, how to get discounts for materials and things. Mike Thynners can help him with all that."

"'Thinners will . . . set things alight,'" Cassie said in the same dreamy voice.

Uncle Guy frowned. "What? Well, yes, he will get things moving, set

82

things alight, as you say. In fact I said the very same thing to Miss Cartwright yesterday when I told her what I planned to suggest to Mr McNeil."

Cassie looked dazed. "But – but you wanted to buy his cottage, you said you did."

"Quite right," Uncle Guy said. "But he wouldn't sell, would he? And on Monday, after he'd turned me down again, he showed me round his workshop, told me what he was trying to do. Well, I got to thinking that perhaps I was banging my head against a brick wall trying to persuade him to sell, especially when I learned the cottage belonged to his uncle. I decided that if I couldn't beat him I might as well help him."

"You – you did?"

83

"I was impressed, Cassie. He deserves to succeed, and I like to help people get on, the way others helped me in the past. Most successful business people do."

"Not Desma Blane," Cassie muttered to herself.

"Desma Blane?" Uncle Guy repeated. "Who is she? Somebody I should know?"

"Er – no." Cassie swallowed twice, then said, "How do you *spell* the name of your accountant?"

It was obviously the last question Uncle Guy was expecting, but he told her just the same.

"Oh," Cassie said. "With a Y."

After that, Uncle Guy talked about the school where Cassie would go whilst she and her mother were in Hartleigh Heights, about how he thought he might want Mrs Bond to stay on anyway because his old book-keeper didn't think she'd be coming back now, not after she'd had her baby, but Cassie heard little of it.

The signature tune of *Blane's Park*

floated around in her head, and she could see the faces of Desma Blane, Tabitha Slygh and the others. They didn't seem quite so *real* any more.

And, in a way, Cassie was glad. Glad that real people didn't behave that way.

"Do you like TV?" Uncle Guy was asking, nodding at the man in wellington boots who was still talking about tractors.

"What? Oh – yes." Cassie stopped, a long considering pause. "At least . . . "

Perhaps it was time to mix with more real people, she thought. Perhaps she'd been wrong to rely on those TV faces to take the place of proper friends. Perhaps it was time to swap Desma Blane and company for some actual living, breathing *people*.

Like Paul McNeil, for starters. Cassie had the feeling Paul would never have watched *Blane's Park* in his life. He was much too interested in everything that

87

was happening to him and his dad to be bothered about a lot of TV characters.

"What sort of programmes do you like?" Uncle Guy asked, making conversation.

"Er . . . quiz games," Cassie told him.